Hawai'i Volcanoes
National Park

In Hawai'i Volcanoes National Park, primal forces of volcanism generate a dynamic cycle of destruction and renewal. Here, on two of the most active volcanoes on Earth, lava flows erase verdant landscapes. This is a natural catastrophe followed by new life.

*T*he violent interaction of molten lava
with the sea produces both black sand
beaches and solid land that extends
the island. Hawai´i Volcanoes National Park
is a park that continues to grow.

Hawai'i Volcanoes National Park was established in 1916 on the island of Hawai'i to protect the geologic, biologic, and cultural resources on Kīlauea and Mauna Loa, Hawai'i's two most active volcanoes

Front cover: Volcanic gases propel lava skyward in a spectacular fountain that may last minutes or hours. Photo by Jeffrey Judd. **Inside front cover:** Dense thickets of uluhe, or false staghorn fern. Photo by Jeff Gnass. **Page 1:** This male 'amakihi, a native Hawaiian honeycreeper. Photo by Jack Jeffrey. **Pages 2/3:** In 1992 lava flows covered Kamoamoa, erasing all traces of this bay. Photo by Peter French. **Pages 4/5:** A curtain of fire penetrates the night sky. Photo by Greg Vaughn.

Edited by Maryellen Conner.
Book Design by K. C. DenDooven.

Twelfth Printing, 2012 • Newest Version

in pictures HAWAI'I VOLCANOES Nature's Continuing Story®
© 1992 KC PUBLICATIONS, INC.

"in pictures... Nature's Continuing Story®"; and the Eagle / Flag icon are registered in the U.S. Patent and Trademark Office.

LC 92-71531. ISBN 978-0-88714-069-3.

in pictures
Hawai'i Volcanoes
Nature's Continuing Story®

by Richard A. Rasp

During RICHARD RASP's 30-year career with the National Park Service, he was involved with the interpretation of many areas including: Shenandoah, Hot Springs, Pinnacles, Everglades, Redwood, and Hawai'i Volcanoes. Dick is also the author of *Redwood: The Story Behind the Scenery*.

The Hawai'i Volcanoes Story

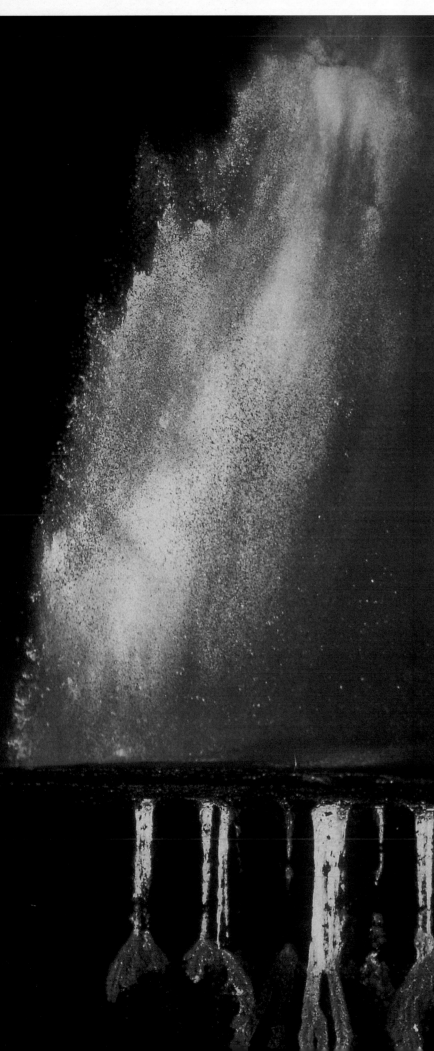

DONALD REESER

All the Hawaiian Islands are built up from volcanic activity. It is a process still going on today—literally. If you were to measure from the ocean floor to the top of Mauna Loa, it could arguably be the second highest mountain in the world. (Mauna Kea would be higher by 117 feet.)

Within **Hawai'i Volcanoes National** Park there are two active volcanic fields. New land is being formed daily as lava flows into the ocean, solidifies and becomes part of the island. In the same manner all Hawaiian Islands were built up this way over millions of years.

Centuries ago people, birds, insects, animals all arrived to propagate the Hawaiian Islands, our 50th state. The National Park is a living, breathing example of geology on the move.

The Hawaiian culture is richly steeped in tradition and legend. A much defined system of life was in place when the white man "discovered" the islands. There are places within the park where you can see not only the early day Hawaiian but the pioneers who arrived and added their contributions.

We can see and appreciate many unique elements of nature within the park boundaries. From the nēnē, the Hawaiian goose, the silversword, to the happyface spider—there are many birds, flowers, even trees that only grow on the islands. Some of these are really only visible now thanks to the protection of the National Park Areas, Hawai'i Volcanoes and Haleakalā on Maui.

Fountains of lava up to 1,780 feet high roared from Kīlauea's east rift zone during the Mauna Ulu eruption. Beginning in May 1969, the eruption continued for over five years. Episodic high fountains produced lava flows that poured into and eventually filled 'Alo'i and 'Alae craters near the main vent.

DANN ESPY

A family of nēnē, the endangered Hawaiian state bird, faces many perils. Populations are declining by introduced mongooses and cats, and being run over by vehicles. Nēnē are especially vulnerable when their young are not old enough to fly.

This is a park to learn from, a place to see the on going shift between forces. With the proper safeguards you can get surprisingly close to an active lava flow.

It is for these reasons that the park was designated as an International Biosphere Reserve back in 1980 and a World Heritage Site in 1987.

And yet, virtually the entire park is accessible. Most places can be seen from designated roadways, hiking is an activity that can allow you to cover more of the more intimate details of this park.

Geology is alive and doing well at Hawai´i Volcanoes National Park.

K.C. DenDooven
Publisher

G. BRAD LEWIS

When flows are accessible, you can experience the awesome spectacle of lava close up and in relative safety.

A Land is Forged

Lava fountains, characteristic of Hawaiian-type eruptions, result from gases that propel incandescent lava skyward. In June 1984, a Pu'u 'Ō'ō fountain reached 1,500 feet in height.

In the photographer's words, this lava dome fountain was an "awesome, rare, silent, and surprising event." A giant volcanic bubble this phenomenon lasts only as long as there is a steady flow of lava and a low, even pressure of gas. It reflects a balance between the upward pressure of magma and the conduit below and the ponded lava from which the fountain rises.

From Beneath the Sea

When lava flows under water its pillow-like shape is determined by the chilling effect of the surrounding seawater. An insulating crust forms, and the pillows may gradually cool without exploding. These scuba-diving photographers are in far greater danger by being hit by falling pillow lava during the landslide than of being burned by the hot water near the molten lava.

G. BRAD LEWIS

Island Building – A Long Process

Volcanoes demonstrate the dynamic nature of our planet, providing evidence of the primal forces of change. About 60 miles beneath the island of Hawai'i, heat from a "hot spot" deep within the Earth, produces molten rock called magma and forces it upward where it is stored in reservoirs less than two miles under the summits. When pressure builds sufficiently, magma rises through conduits to the summits or along rift zones (areas of weakness) radiating from the summit. Mauna Loa and Kīlauea in Hawai'i are shield volcanoes, unlike stratovolcanoes such as Mount St. Helens, Fuji, and Vesuvius. The more fluid and less gaseous Hawaiian lava often flows long distances, laying down successive layers to form a broad shield. Like pages of a book, hundreds of thousands of lava flows were laid down to build Mauna Loa over 32,000 feet from the sea floor up to its present altitude of 13,677 feet. Mauna Loa and Kīlauea rate high among the most hazardous volcanoes in the world. Major earthquakes, massive landslides, and explosive steam eruptions that devastate large areas can all occur with little warning, and reveal the power that changes these dramatic landscapes.

A lava lake forms over an active magma conduit when lava builds a levee that contains a molten pond. The lake surface cools and makes a crust, much like the skin in a kettle of boiled milk. Movements of lava beneath this "skin" cause cracks that separate the surface into plates. In studying the plate patterns, geologists have found analogies to the tectonic plates of the Earth.

Lava emerging from a fissure or vent is often expelled forcefully by spattering. It solidifies to form a circular spatter cone or a ridge-like spatter rampart—or it coats the surrounding area in an erratic manner.

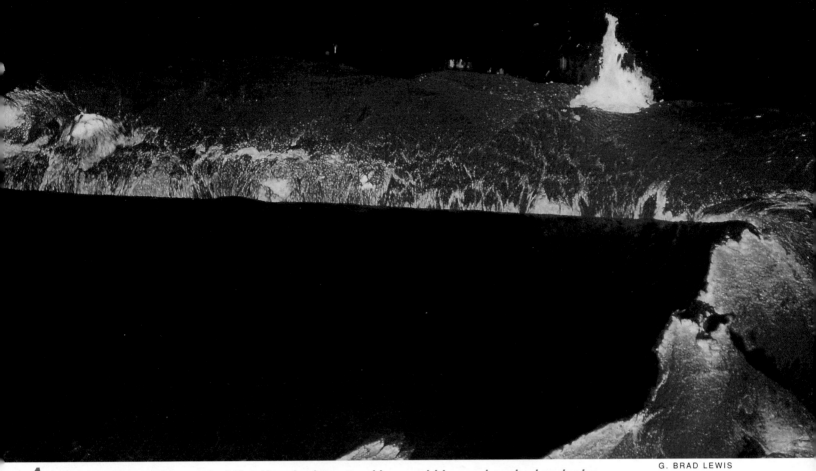

A cooled section of the crust of Kupaianaha lava pond is overridden and pushed under by fresh molten lava. This once active pond, now a solidified shield, was the source of lava that for several years flowed through a seven-mile tube system to the seashore. On its way it destroyed several villages and numerous homes, but added about 300 acres to the island.

the billowy pāhoehoe lava succumbs to the the mighty force of the ´a´ā flow

Molten ʻaʻā lava overrides pāhoehoe. Both types of lava have the same chemical composition, but are formed under different conditions. In its molten state the rough, jagged, clinkery ʻaʻā has less gas, is less fluid, and has a lower temperature than the smooth, billowy pāhoehoe.

As molten pāhoehoe moves, the more fluid lava underneath carries its partially solidified "skin" molding wrinkles and swirls.

Molten Rock on the Move

PETER FRENCH

Along the cooler edges of a river of molten lava, levees of solidified lava build and meet in the center to eventually form a tube. Lava stays hot enough to travel several miles through these insulated conduits.

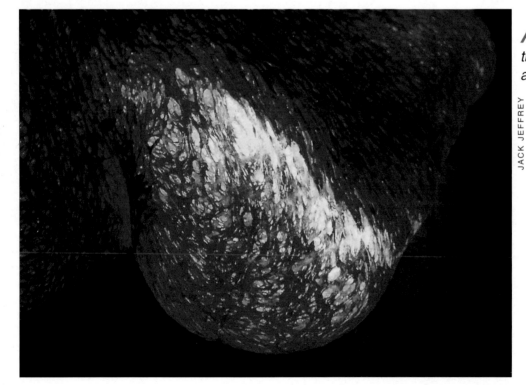

JACK JEFFREY

An inflating lava toe marks the advancing front of an active flow.

JOHN KJARGAARD

On the slope of Pu'u 'Ō 'ō an active fissure served as a conduit that fed a lava pond. Fortunately for the videographer standing above the cauldron, the sulfurous fumes are blowing away from him.

Molten Lava Makes its Journey to the Sea

SHARKBAIT PRODUCTIONS

An active flow overruns a coastal forest, consuming everything in its path. Methane gas generated by plants often concentrates in pockets beneath the forest floor. When ignited by lava it may explode, blasting away overlying rocks. These small but powerful detonations occur without warning, so visitors should avoid vegetated areas with active flows.

As hot lava flows into the ocean, small stream explosions propel tephra (airborne lava) upward. Highly acidic fumes called "laze" (lava haze) are produced when the molten lava contact ocean water.

Not much will stop lava flowing downhill. Since 1987, when lava first poured into the ocean, a little more than 600 acres of new land has been added to the island.

Lava Landscapes

DORIAN WEISEL

Mauna Ulu forms a link in the chain of craters that characterizes part of the east rift zone. This zone of weakness in the Earth's crust extends 35 miles from Kīlauea Caldera to beyond the eastern tip of the island of Hawai'i. Magma, which is constantly replenished from deep within the Earth's mantle, travels from a pressurized storage chamber beneath Kīlauea Caldera through a complex system of conduits to the east rift zone. There it may emerge as lava through fissures.

PETER FRENCH

Pit craters are formed by the collapse of overlying rock into a reservoir that once contained magma. The wall of this pit crater displays layers of lava built up over thousands of years to form a shield volcano.

ED COOPER

Moku´āweoweo Caldera occupies the summit of Mauna Loa, an active volcano that last erupted in 1984. During the growth of Hawaiian volcanoes, the tops collapse forming large craters known as calderas. Mauna Loa is a classic example of a shield volcano and the largest volcano on Earth.

In 1959, enthralled spectators saw lava erupt from a fissure in the wall of Kīlauea Iki Crater. Its fountain reached a record 1,900 feet. Air-blown cinder formed Pu´u Pua´i (fountaining hill), and devastated forest as much as three miles away.

ED COOPER

G. BRAD LEWIS

Thurston Lava Tube (Nāhuku) formed 500 to 550 years ago when a channelized lava flow crusted over. When the eruption stopped, the hot fluid core drained away.

GREG VAUGHN

Hot, magmatic gases rising beneath Sulphur Banks cool and react with the atmosphere upon reaching the surface and precipitate delicate sulfur crystals. Sulfur gases are dangerous to human health. Persons with respiratory or heart problems, infants, young children, and pregnant women should avoid the Sulphur Banks and Halemaʻumaʻu areas.

JOHN KJARGAARD

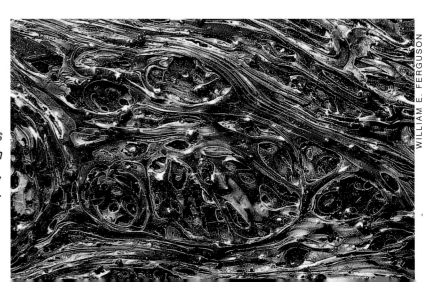

WILLIAM E. FERGUSON

A close-up view of pāhoehoe lava reveals glassy threads of translucent basalt, the main type of Hawaiian rock. Basalt is about half silica, the element from which glass is made.

...even nature can be caught off-guard by pele's wrath

*F*luid pāhoehoe lava often quickly surrounds a living tree and chills to form a sheath of solidified lava. As surrounding molten lava drains away, a "lava tree" remains.

*W*hen the ceiling of a lava tube collapses, a "skylight" is formed that provides a view of molten lava inside the tube. A complex network of lava tubes underlie the surface of Hawaiian volcanoes. During active flows, newly-formed tubes insulate the lava, allowing it to retain its heat and travel several miles. This produces gently sloping terrain.

JEFFREY JUDD

WILLIAM E. FERGUSON

Life After Lava–Rebuilding a Forest

An aerial view of Kīlauea volcano reveals a patchwork of lava fields and forest or shrubland. Lava flows often surround and isolate areas of vegetation, creating ecological islands called kīpuka. Some areas have escaped lava flows for several hundred years and support mature forests. Other areas recently overrun by lava must begin the process of renewal on a barren landscape. Native plants and animals have adapted to this cycle of destruction and rebirth. About 95 percent of the land on Kīlauea Volcano has been covered by lava flows within the last 1,000 years. Along the east rift zone, where most of the recent lava flows have been, rainfall is high and plants can begin re-colonizing in less than a year. First to arrive are algae and lichens, which grow best in crevices that provide shade and collect water and wind-blown particles. Ferns and mosses are next, followed by grasses, shrubs,

and trees. Life begets more life as each pioneer improves living conditions by helping to accumulate soil and hold more moisture. Once trees such as ´ōhi´a gain a foothold, the colonization process accelerates. When tree roots penetrate new lava tubes, another habitat is opened for colonization. Under the right conditions of temperature and humidity, a fascinating world of insects and spiders is able to flourish in total darkness. Roots serve as underground connections, a sort of umbilical cord that supplies nutrients from the surface above. Plant hoppers feed on the roots. They in turn are eaten by other troglodyte (cave dwellers). Blind crickets are eaten by blind big-eyed hunting spiders. In less than a hundred years these lava tubes can be covered by a lush forest of ´ōhi´a and tree ferns, completing the cycle of rebirth after a lava flow.

...Kīlauea's
calm before
the storm

Barring another lava flow, by the time this girl becomes an adult, a native forest may have formed here.

Even when not erupting, Kīlauea displays ample evidence that its repose is only temporary. At Steaming Bluffs hot rocks just beneath the surface create steam from surface water, allowing only shallow-rooted plants to thrive.

Overleaf : A lava "bench" or shelf builds as lava pours into the sea. Under its own weight a section may suddenly break, revealing a lava cascade. Photo by G. Brad Lewis.

G. BRAD LEWIS

Forest Regeneration

The process of converting new lava into soil is affected by the type of lava, level of moisture, and amount of plant growth. The rough surface of 'a'ā lava provides more shady growing sites for young plants than pāhoehoe. Those areas where the sun is intense and rainfall minimal produce relatively shallow soils over a very long period. However, in cloudy and wet mountain areas soils are deeper and form more quickly. With enough rainfall young 'ōhi'a trees grow rapidly, soon forming a closed canopy that improves growing conditions for plants that cannot tolerate full sun. In the moist soil and dappled sunlight, tree ferns, 'ama'u ferns and other native plants thrive.

An 'ōhi'a lehua tree, eternal optimist and one of the most versatile trees in the park, grows out of a crack in Hōlei Pali. The pali (cliffs) formed when stresses created by magma moving through the rift zone and the force of gravity caused the south flank of Kīlauea to slip seaward along a fault.

A grove of young koa trees reclaims the land once covered by lava. One of the largest trees in Hawai'i, koa is found nowhere else in the world. They form dense groves in kīpuka (tree islands) along the Mauna Loa Strip Road. In the park they are protected from grazing animals. Hawaiians highly value koa wood mainly for canoe making, building materials, and surfboards.

PHILIP ROSENBERG

G. BRAD LEWIS

Life is only temporary in this earthquake-caused crack on the edge of Kīlauea Caldera. The next major earthquake, perhaps generated by the tremendous pressure of moving magma, may cause this section of wall to collapse into the caldera. You can see ample evidence of earthquakes in the Kīlauea summit area.

ED COOPER

Lichen and ferns are among the first plants to grow in new lava because they can endure the harsh conditions of intense sunlight. 'A'ā lava provides a better growing medium than pāhoehoe because its rough texture collects more humus and provides more shade in its numerous sheltered cracks.

G. BRAD LEWIS

A Flowering of Life

Forty million years or more of isolation produced a biological paradise in the Hawaiian Islands. Diverse habitats and ecological niches engendered a fascinating array of plants and animals. Getting to these remote islands was not easy. Life reached the island by wing, wind, or wave. Birds carried hitchhiking seeds; the winds blew in spores, seeds, and insects; and ocean currents brought buoyant, salt-resistant seeds and floated rafts of debris that carried insects. The few hardy pioneers that survived the often harsh conditions adapted to a variety of new ecological niches, from tropical to alpine. In long isolation from their homeland relatives, plants and animals evolved into new life forms. From 272 flowering plant immigrants, at least 1,000 evolved. From 300 to 400 ancestral arthropods, 6,000 to 10,000 species were created. Sixteen land birds evolved into at least 100 species. Ninety percent or more of these new species are found only in the Hawaiian Islands. Over millions of years the process of evolution was unimpeded. Hawai'i became a showcase of evolution that would have provided Charles Darwin with many more examples of natural selection than the Galapagos Islands to support his *Origin of Species.*

Nēnē, the Hawaiian goose, probably evolved from an ancestral Canada goose. The reduced webbing between its toes, compared to other geese, is an adaptation to life on the lava flows. Until alien predators such as mongooses and cats arrived in Hawai'i, nēnē populations numbered in the tens of thousands. Today, the park fences large breeding areas to protect them from predators.

JEFF GNASS

A grove of 'ōhi'a, kukui, hao, and lama trees mantles the slopes of Hōlei Pali surrounded by pāhoehoe and 'a'ā flows. The invasion of foreign grasses poses a new danger to these trees because, unlike native grasses, they are more dense and burn more intensely. Today, fires caused by lava or people are larger and more frequent, threatening many native trees and shrubs.

Diversity of Life

Splashy yellow flowers of the māmane adorn the park landscape. Seed pods of this legume nourish the endangered palila bird.

JACK JEFFREY

WILLIAM P. MULL

One of three native tree ferns, the meu occurs only on the island of Hawai'i. It may reach 40 feet under ideal conditions in the 'Ōla'a forest.

RICHARD A. RASP

Young koa seedlings and root sprouts produce true leaves typical of other acacias. As they mature, crescent-shaped and flattened leaf stalks called phyllodes replace their precursors. Some botanists think phyllodes resist moisture loss and thus enhance survival of koa.

RICHARD A. RASP

Hawaiians prize maile for its fragrant aroma and decorative value when used as a lei. In Hawaiian tradition, long garlands of maile heralded peace between warring chiefs. Like other native plants, it is protected within the park.

A lichen-covered koa symbolizes a healthy and diverse environment. The park provides a refuge for old-growth koa forests and their associated species, which are rapidly being depleted on private lands by logging and cattle ranching. Cattle relish tender young koa, killing future replacements for the older trees. Human demand for the high-quality hardwood has caused the destruction of thousands of acres of irreplaceable koa forests. For several native birds, including the endangered 'akiapōlā'au, old-growth koa forests provide vital habitats.

JOHN KJARGAARD

JACK JEFFREY

*T*hrough evolution this "mintless mint" lost its ancestors' characteristic aroma, a defensive mechanism that helped repel herbivores in the mint's former mainland habitat.

Flora Uniquely Hawaiian

*T*he endangered Ka'ū silversword, a relative of the sunflower, occurs only on the slopes of Mauna Loa, where it has adapted to harsh sunlight, limited rainfall, and dry air. A dense covering of hair produces a silvery sheen on the leaves, while providing protection from sunlight and dehydration. Each stem flowers only once.

PHOTOS BY JACK JEFFREY

Fiddleheads unfurl from the tops of stately tree ferns unique to Hawai´i. Hāpu´u (left and right) may grow to 20 feet high and 3 feet in diameter, with fronds 12 feet long. Silky fluff called pulu that covers young fronds and the top of trunks was used by early Hawaiians as an absorbent dressing for wounds and as an embalming material. ´Ama´u ferns (center) grow smaller than hāpu´u and their new fronds are typically red.

JOHN KJARGAARD

Hawaiians call this rare and endemic plant ʻōhai. This member of the pea family has a small population in the Ka´ū Desert.

This endemic and critically endangered hau kuahiwi, relative of the hibiscus, has tubular flowers that co-evolved with and matched the curved beaks of certain Hawaiian honeycreepers.

JACK JEFFREY

PETER FRENCH

The 'io, Hawaiian hawk, is found nowhere else but on Hawai'i Island. It is endangered due to loss of habitat.

JACK JEFFREY

An 'i'iwi forms a dazzling silhouette as he perches on a native raspberry. This Hawaiian honeycreeper evolved a long sickle-shaped bill ideal for gathering nectar from long curved flowers.

JACK JEFFREY

'Apapane, one of the commonest native honeycreepers, may be seen sipping nectar from 'ōhi'a lehua flowers in Kīlauea area forests. Like other honeycreepers, the 'apapane evolved from an ancestral finch. The descendants of this colonizer adapted to various ecological opportunities and formed new species.

...from # grinning arachnids to # glowering hawks.

JACK D. SWENSON

White-tailed tropicbirds nest in the steep cliffs of Halema´uma´u Crater and fly to the coast to catch fish.

JACK JEFFREY

Kamehameha butterflies are one of two endemic species. Their larval caterpillars thrive on māmaki trees where they are threatened by alien Japanese white eye birds.

WILLIAM P. MULL

A smiling face awaits an inquisitive visitor who peers under a rainforest leaf. Happyface spiders reach a mere one-quarter inch long, and no two individuals have the same markings. This species is found only on Hawai'i Island.

Green sea turtles live along Hawai'i's coast, but nest in the state's Northwestern Islands. The endangered Hawksbill turtle, a smaller species, nests on Hawai'i's southern coast.

PHILIP ROSENBERG

A Land of Great Diversity

RICHARD A. RASP

A 7.2 magnitude earthquake awakened 32 campers at Halapē just before dawn on November 29, 1975. The coast dropped over ten feet, generating a tsunami that swept through the area, killing two people. Most survivors were tossed inland into an old lava crack by the second of two sea waves.

G. BRAD LEWIS

'Ākala, a Hawaiian raspberry evolving without large herbivores, has fewer thorns than its mainland ancestors.

Native tree ferns line the trail near the entrance to Thurston Lava Tube (Nāhuku). This Hawaiian rain forest is an especially good place to hear the songs of native birds such as 'apapane, 'ōma'o, and 'amakihi.

JACK JEFFREY

Hawaiians found the hard wood of the native 'a'ali'i useful for making digging sticks and house posts. Leaves and green-to-red fruit capsules are still used for dyes and lei.

Hairgrass, endemic to Hawai'i, grows in the park's upper elevations. This bunchgrass forms a dense ground cover, and often grows with bracken fern. It probably arrived in Hawai'i millions of years ago as a hitchhiker on the muddy feet of a migrating bird.

When you leave the lush rain forest surrounding Kīlauea Visitor Center and travel west along the Crater Rim Drive, the scenery drastically changes as you enter the Ka'ū Desert. On this leeward side of Kīlauea, rainfall is reduced by more than one-half. Life is harsh here because of hot, dry conditions and acidic fumes emitted and blown downwind from Halema'uma'u Crater.

*An offering, or ho´okupu, is made to appease
Pele, the goddess of volcanoes. A gift of food
is wrapped with ti leaves, and tied with
a garland of ´ōhi‘a lehua.*

An Historical Perspective

When Polynesians first landed on the Hawaiian Islands about 1,600 years ago, they encountered a primeval landscape. Survival was not easy in this new land more than 2,400 miles from their home. They brought a few plants that provided food, fiber, and medicine, and began clearing coastal forests for cultivation. These pioneers developed a farming society that was supplemented by fishing. From their forefathers they brought language and traditions upon which society was based. As there was not written language, chants provided the means of transferring knowledge to new generations. Through chants Hawaiians communicated to their gods, including Pele, the goddess of volcanoes. Structure in their feudal society came from a kapu system of sacred people, places, things, and times. A detailed code regulated the behavior of maka´āinana, commoners, as well as the ali‘i, or chiefs.

*Petroglyphs chipped
in 500- to 700-year-
old pāhoehoe lava
near the park's coast
may tell symbolic
stories, but what
these rock carvings
actually mean is
uncertain.*

*W*aha'ula Heiau, "Temple of the Red Mouth," was built about 700 years ago as the first luakini heiau (temple) in Hawai'i. Here Hawaiian royalty ordered human sacrifices to seek the favor of Kū, one of their gods. This practice ended in the early 1800s when the kapu system was abolished. Lava flowed through this area several times during the summer of 1989 and later, leaving the ruins of a visitor center (in the background, to the right) as testimony to the unpredictability of Pele. In 1997, she finally conquered, and lava buried the entire temple complex site.

*P*ulu, a silky reddish-brown fluff that grows on tree ferns, was harvested in great quantities during the mid to late 1800s for use as stuffing in pillows and mattresses. It was processed here at the pulu factory before being transported to the coast for shipment to foreign markets.

OLD PULU FACTORY

BETWEEN 1851 AND 1884 GREAT QUANTITIES OF PULU, THE SOFT, REDDISH-BROWN FIBER COVERING THE COILED FRONDS OF THE TREE FERN (HAPUU), WERE HARVESTED ON HAWAII. MUCH OF IT WAS PROCESSED WITHIN THESE WALLS, LATER TO BE SHIPPED FROM KEAUHOU LANDING TO FOREIGN MARKETS FOR USE AS STUFFING IN PILLOWS AND MATTRESSES.

Showy pink flowers of the banana poka belie the destructive effect that this alien has on native forests. Fast growing vines often smother trees that are important to native birds. To help control this pest, scientists have released a moth whose larvae eat poka flower buds.

RICHARD A. RASP

Alien Invaders Bring Trouble to Paradise

For eons island life had evolved new species that could best utilize available habitats and ecological niches. However, with specialization they lost many of the defense mechanisms possessed by their ancestors. Their isolation from continental competitors and predators ended about 1,600 years ago with the arrival of Polynesian settlers who brought pigs, dogs, jungle fowl, and a variety of plants in order to survive. Captain Cook's landing in 1778 marked the beginning of a new alien invasion that included European pigs, goats, and cattle. Later immigrants intentionally or accidentally brought European rats, cats, mongoose, mosquitoes, ants, wasps, and several food and ornamental plants. Now the rapid influx and establishment of alien species is threatening the existence of native species and changing the conditions that for millions of years fostered the evolution of Hawai'i's unique ecosystems. Aggressive alien plants smother or displace native vegetation. Introduced animals destroy native forests, eat or compete with indigenous species, and spread foreign diseases. This alien invasion, along with habitat destruction, is responsible for the demise of nearly 50 percent of Hawai'i's native birds, as well as numerous other plants and animals.

Introduced as an ornamental, kāhili ginger thickly carpets the forest floor, displacing native understory plants.

RICHARD A. RASP

RICHARD A. RASP

The prolific faya tree produces many fruits. It is the most serious threat to park forests, growing to 50 feet tall and forming dense strands that displace understory plants.

...the survival of the fittest on display

JACK JEFFREY

*T*he abundant Japanese white eye, an alien bird, competes with native birds for nectar and insects. Large flocks glean caterpillars of the native Kamehameha butterfly from māmaki trees. Whiteyes also eat the fruits of the introduced faya tree and spread the seeds over large areas of the park.

*M*ongoose pups have steel-blue eyes that eventually change to the auburn-colored eyes of the adult. Mongoose was brought from Jamaica in 1883 to reduce rats in sugarcane fields. Today they are a serious predator on the eggs and goslings of the endangered nēnē and other birds.

JACK JEFFREY

*F*eral pigs (formerly domesticated but now wild) cause tremendous damage to native forests and their inhabitants. Besides eating many endangered plants, these hoofed rototillers create opening that encourage the spread of alien plants. Pigs carve out depressions that collect rainwater, allowing mosquitoes to breed. Mosquitoes transmit bird malaria to native birds.

DANN ESPY

The Park Today

RICHARD A. RASP

In our quest for superlative park adventures, it is not easy to find an equal to the fiery spectacle of a river of lava passing 20 feet away. The experience of molten lava on the move, the intense heat, the smell of brimstone–all saturate one's senses. It is at once exciting and mesmerizing—a primal experience that you will never forget; but Hawai´i Volcanoes National Park offers more than a drive-in volcano. Those who take the time to explore the frontcountry trails or the backcountry wilderness can discover the spectacular on many levels, whether it is a broad panorama, or a tiny insect. A quiet walk through a rainforest can remind us of our connection to the land, and our responsibility to preserve these resources for present and future generations.

A park ranger-interpreter educates visitors about how Kīlauea Caldera was formed and other aspects of volcanism. Guided walks through rain forests, across lava flows, and to cultural sites help visitors understand and appreciate the park's fascinating natural and cultural resources.

The 1959 Kīlauea Iki eruption covered the forest with cinder. The Devastation Trail was built so visitors could witness the process of forest recovery and regeneration.

G. BRAD LEWIS

*T*he Thomas A. Jaggar Museum is a geological museum dedicated to seismology and volcanology. Several working seismographs and tilt meters depict earthquakes as they occur. There are videos of eruptions and an exhibit of clothing and gear from scientists who got too close to molten lava. The overlook, behind the museum, offers visitors excellent views when Kilauea Caldera vents.

*R*oad builders face a unique challenge maintaining park roads as lava knows no barriers other than gravity. Lava 80 feet or more in depth has covered miles of this road.

*B*icyclists pause for refreshment at a pit crater along Crater Rim Drive. Park roads offer numerous scenic pullouts for leisurely motorists, but bicycling and hiking allow many visitors a more rewarding park experience.

All About Hawai'i Volcanoes

How to Contact Us:

Call us at:

(808) 985-6000

Write to us at:

Hawai'i Volcanoes
National Park
P.O. Box 52
Hawai'i National Park, HI
96718-0052

Fax:

(808) 985-6004

Email:

havo_interpretation@nps.gov

Website:

www.nps.gov/havo

AN 'I'IWI
PHOTO BY JACK JEFFREY

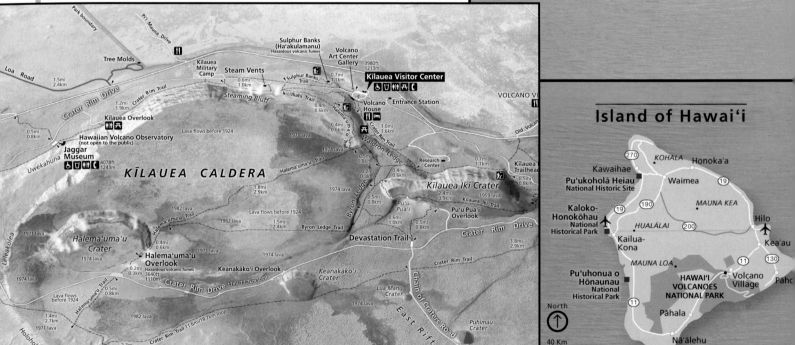

Island of Hawai'i

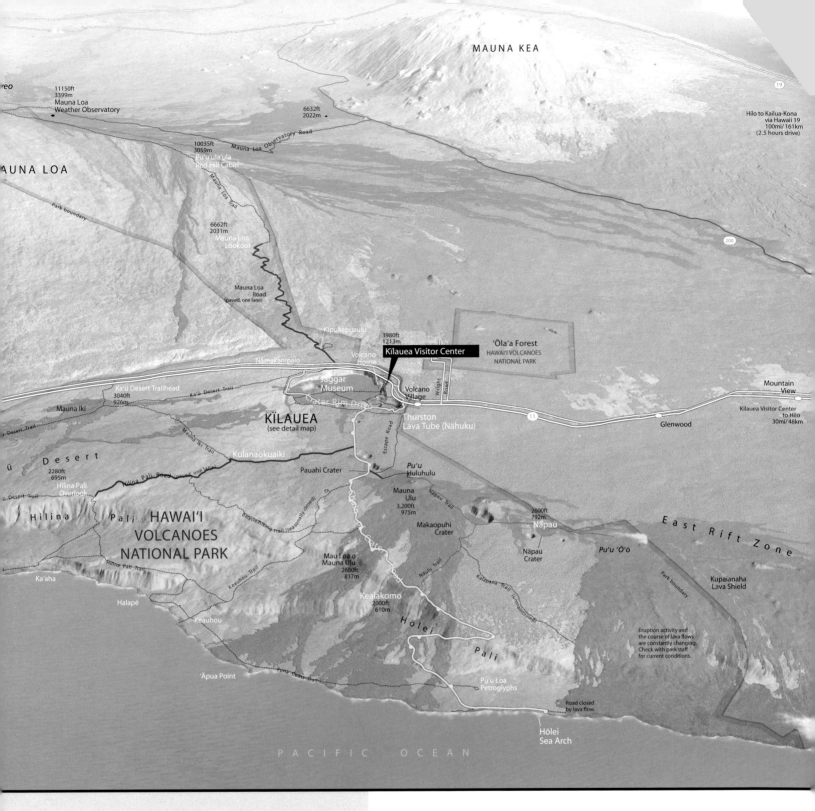

MAUNA KEA

11150ft
3399m
Mauna Loa
Weather Observatory

6632ft
2022m

Hilo to Kailua-Kona
via Hawaii 19
100mi/161km
(2.5 hours drive)

10035ft
3059m
Pu'u'ula'ula
Red Hill Cabin

AUNA LOA

Park boundary

6662ft
2031m
Mauna Loa
Lookout

Mauna Loa
Road
(paved, one lane)

Kīpukapuaulu

3980ft
1213m

'Ōla'a Forest
HAWAI'I VOLCANOES
NATIONAL PARK

Kīlauea Visitor Center

Volcano
House

Mountain
View

Nāmakanipaio

Jaggar
Museum

Ka'ū Desert Trailhead
3040ft
926m

Ka'ū Desert Trail

Crater Rim Drive

Volcano
Village

Kīlauea Visitor Center
to Hilo
30mi/48km

Mauna Iki

KĪLAUEA
(see detail map)

Thurston
Lava Tube (Nāhuku)

Glenwood

Mauna Iki Trail

Kulanaokuaiki

Ka'ū Desert Trail

Pu'u
Huluhulu

Desert

2280ft
695m

Hilina Pali
Overlook

Hilina Pali Road (paved, one lane)

Pauahi Crater

Mauna
Ulu
3,200ft
975m

Nāpau Trail

East Rift Zone

U. Desert Trail

Hilina

Pali

**HAWAI'I
VOLCANOES
NATIONAL PARK**

Bicycle/hiking trail (seasonally closed)

Makaopuhi
Crater

2600ft
792m

Nāpau

Nāpau
Crater

Pu'u 'Ō'ō

Ka'aha

Hilina Pali Trail

Mau Loa o
Mauna Ulu
2680ft
817m

Keauhou Trail

Nāulu Trail

Kalapana Trail (unmaintained)

Park boundary

Kupaianaha
Lava Shield

Halapē

Keauhou

Kealakomo
2000ft
610m

Hōlei

Pali

Eruption activity and
the course of lava flows
are constantly changing.
Check with park staff
for current conditions.

'Āpua Point

Puna Coast Trail

Pu'u Loa
Petroglyphs

Road closed
by lava flow.

Hōlei
Sea Arch

PACIFIC OCEAN

Hawai'i Natural History Association

The Hawai'i Natural History Association was established in 1933. In partnership with the National Park Service, HNHA advocates and promotes the discovery, understanding, appreciations, enjoyment and stewardship of the natural and human history of the National Parks of the Pacific. In addition to Hawai'i Volcanoes National Park, it also serves Haleakalā National Park, Kaloko-Honōkohau National Historical Park, National Park of American Sāmoa, Pu'ukoholā Heiau National Historic site, and Pu'uhonua o Honaunau National Historic Park.

SUGGESTED READING AND MORE

BABB, JANET L. *Hawai'i Volcanoes: The Story Behind the Scenery.* Wickenburg, Arizona: KC Publications, Inc., 1999 (rev.).

DAWS, A. GAVAN. *Shoal of Time.* New York, New York: Macmillan, 1968.

DECKER, ROBERT and BARBARA DECKER. *Volcano Watching.* Hawai'i National Park, Hawai'i: Hawai'i Natural History Association, 1996 (rev.).

HELIKER, CHRISTINA and DORIAN WEISEL. *Kīlauea, The Newest Land on Earth.* Honolulu, Hawai'i: Island Heritage Publishing, 1990.

KUETEMEYER, MICHAEL and ANULA SHETTY. *Explore Kīlauea Volcano* (CD-ROM). Philadelphia, Pennsylvania: Firework Studio, 1997.

STONE, CHARLES P. and LINDA W. PRATT. *Hawai'i's Plants and Animals: Biological Sketches of Hawai'i Volcanoes National Park.* Hawai'i National Park, Hawai'i: Hawai'i Natural History Association, 2001 (rev.).

PETER FRENCH

Hawai'i Volcanoes National Park, located on the newest and largest island of Hawai'i preserves the natural setting of Mauna Loa and Kīlauea volcanoes. Its vast lava fields, lush rain forests and alpine summits offer glimpses into the continuing process of creating land and life. On a tropical volcanic landscape, complex and unique ecosystems and a distinct human culture have evolved. As both a World Heritage Site and an International Biosphere Reserve, the park has achieved international recognition for its outstanding values to humankind.

Pu'u 'Ō'ō (hill of the extinct 'Ō'ō bird) functions as a chimney that vents volcanic gases on Kīlauea's east rift zone. It began forming in January 1983 and reached a maximum height of 835 feet. Ten years later, the cone began falling apart, and today, it is 200 feet shorter than shown in this photo.

Here is a Park that is alive, moving, growing, and evolving.
We see nature's work at Hawai'i Volcanoes National Park.

PETER FRENCH

The chain of Craters Road takes you through a world of its own.
Built upon many lava flows, you will see how molten rock ages,
vegetation begins – how all the islands began and grew.

KC Publications has been the leading publisher of colorful, interpretive books
about National Park areas, public lands, Indian Culture, and related subjects for over 45 years.
We have 5 active series – over 125 titles – with Translation Packages in up to 8 languages
for over half the areas we cover. Write, call, or visit our web site for our full-color catalog.

Our series are:

The Story Behind the Scenery® – Compelling stories of over 65 National Park areas
and similar Public Land areas. Some with Translation Packages.

in pictures... Nature's Continuing Story® – A companion, pictorially oriented, series on
America's National Parks. All titles have Translation Packages.

For Young Adventurers® – Dedicated to young seekers and keepers of all things wild
and sacred. Explore America's Heritage from A to Z.

Voyage of Discovery® – Exploration of the expansion of the western United States.

Indian Culture and the Southwest – All about Native Americans, past and present.

We publish over 125 titles – Books and other related specialty products.
Our full-color catalog is available online or by contacting us:
Call (800) 626-9673, Fax (928) 684-5189, Write to the address below,
Or visit our web site at www.nationalparksbooks.com

Published by KC Publications • P.O. Box 3615 • Wickenburg, AZ 85358

Inside back cover: The
red glow of lava cascading
into the ocean mesmerizes
those fortunate enough
to experience it up close.
Photo by G. Brad Lewis

Back cover: Lava pours into
the sea. The "Big Island"
Continues to GROW!
Photo by Brad Lewis.

Created, Designed, and Published in the U.S.A.
Printed by Tien Wah Press (Pte.) Ltd, Singapore
Pre-Press by United Graphic Pte. Ltd